Life Lessons from My Cat

Print ISBN 978-1-62416-679-2

Cover design by Greg Jackson, Thinkpen Design

Published by Barbour Publishing, Inc., P.O. Box 719, Uhrichsville, Ohio 44683, www.barbourbooks.com

Our mission is to publish and distribute inspirational products offering exceptional value and biblical encouragement to the masses.

Member of the
Evangelical Christian
Publishers Association

Printed in China.

Life Lessons from My Cat

Betty Ost-Everley

INSPIRATION FOR CAT LOVERS

BARBOUR
PUBLISHING

Contents

Introduction

My three cats amaze me! Each has its own idiosyncrasies, personality, likes and dislikes. I look at them—Frick, Yoda, and Chewy—and wonder what the Creator had in mind when they were being shaped in their mothers' wombs. Maybe similar thoughts as when we were created? These beautiful four-legged examples of His handiwork teach me daily more about Him. God is present in each living thing, and His lessons are there to be learned, if we are only open to them. I am thankful that many of His lessons come softly, on padded, furry feet.

There's No Place
Like Home

"My Father's house has many rooms;
if that were not so, would I have told
you that I am going there to
prepare a place for you? And if I go and
prepare a place for you, I will come
back and take you to be with me that
you also may be where I am."

JOHN 14:2-3 NIV

All of our cats were born in the wilds of our backyard and had feral parents. The idea of coming inside to live was an odd idea to them at first. It was a maze of rooms that contained frightening things. The television and vacuum cleaner were two foreign objects that caused our cats to go into hiding. Eventually, they got used to everything, and Frick even watches television now. Where we live is now their home, a place they associate with being fed and cared for. They know that their "forever home" means love.

Jesus talked about our "forever home" and described it as a real place where we would live with Him someday. He has lovingly prepared it for our arrival, and we will feel nothing but the love our heavenly Father has for us.

When I was a small girl, I had a cat named April. April had a litter box, litter, food dishes, food, and water. Now I realize how deprived she was! Today's felines have condos, trees, towers, hammocks, cradles, playhouses, and tunnels. Some even have cat-sized sofas, chairs, and beds. Yet April loved me well, even in her poverty.

UNKNOWN

It's really the cat's house—
we just pay the mortgage.

UNKNOWN

Good cat owners always introduce their cats
as members of the family.

I have learned a lot from my cat. When life
is loud and scary, go under the bed and nap.
When you want someone to notice you,
sit on the book that person is reading.
And if someone sits in your chair,
glare at her until she moves.

Any household with at least one feline
member has no need for an alarm clock.

LOUISE A. BELCHER

In peace I will lie down and sleep, for you alone, Lord, make me dwell in safety.

PSALM 4:8 NIV

Even though I walk through the darkest valley, I will fear no evil, for you are with me; your rod and your staff, they comfort me.

PSALM 23:4 NIV

Sin pays off with death. But God's gift is eternal life given by Jesus Christ our Lord.

ROMANS 6:23 CEV

For we know that if the earthly tent we live in is destroyed, we have a building from God, an eternal house in heaven, not built by human hands.

2 CORINTHIANS 5:1 NIV

Cats sleep anywhere,
any table, any chair.
Top of piano, window ledge,
in the middle, on the edge.
Open drawer, empty shoe,
anybody's lap will do.
Fitted in a cardboard box,
in the cupboard with your frocks.
Anywhere! They don't care!
Cats sleep anywhere.

ELEANOR FARJEON

"In My Father's house are many mansions;
if it were not so, I would have told you.
I go to prepare a place for you. And if I go
and prepare a place for you, I will come again
and receive you to Myself; that where I am,
there you may be also."

JOHN 14:2-3 NKJV

What little things bring you joy? They are different for each of us. . . .when I really feel listened to. . . when my son gives me a big hug and holds on tight. . . . Make your own list— and then be sure to indulge regularly.

SUSANNAH SETON

Live wholeheartedly. Be surprised!
Give thanks and praise!
Then you will discover the
fullness of your life.

BROTHER DAVID STEINDL RASE

Cat hair on my best coat,
Even on the mouse!
You live and eat and breathe cat hair,
When cats live in your house.

UNKNOWN

Cats seem to go on the principle that it never
does any harm to ask for what you want.

JOSEPH WOOD KRUTCH

Cats, no less liquid than their shadows
Offer no angles to the wind.
They slip, diminished, neat, through loopholes
Less than themselves. . .

A. S. J. TESSIMOND

The really great thing about cats
is their endless variety. One can pick a
cat to fit almost any kind of decor, color,
scheme, income, personality, mood. But
under the fur, whatever color it may be,
there still lies, essentially unchanged,
one of the world's free souls.

ERIC GURNEY

Places to look: behind the books in the bookshelf, any cupboard with a gap too small for any cat to squeeze through, the top of anything sheer, under anything too low for a cat to squash under and inside the piano.

ROSEANNE AMBROSE-BROWN

Ever consider what pets must think of us? I mean, here we come back from a grocery store with the most amazing haul—chicken, pork, half a cow. They must think we're the greatest hunters on earth!

ANNE TYLER

Jesus answered, "Everyone who drinks this water will be thirsty again, but whoever drinks the water I give them will never thirst. Indeed, the water I give them will become in them a spring of water welling up to eternal life."

JOHN 4:13–14 NIV

Be my mighty rock, the place where I can always run for protection. Save me by your command! You are my mighty rock and my fortress.

PSALM 71:3 CEV

As you know, we count as blessed those who have persevered. You have heard of Job's perseverance and have seen what the Lord finally brought about. The Lord is full of compassion and mercy.

JAMES 5:11 NIV

My cat the clown: paying no mind to whom he should impress. Merely living his life, doing what pleases him, and making me smile.

UNKNOWN

Who among us hasn't envied a cat's ability to ignore the cares of daily life and to relax completely?

KAREN BRADEMEYER

Companions
elusive at times
invasive at others
not wanting to be bothered
except to further
their own agendas;
a place to sleep
food
occasional warmth
and attention.
Small furry people
they seem to be
in their selfishness
but smarter
because
nothing is expected.

BESS KEMP

And my God shall supply all your need according to His riches in glory by Christ Jesus.

PHILIPPIANS 4:19 NKJV

Trust in the LORD with all your heart, and lean not on your own understanding; in all your ways acknowledge Him, and He shall direct your paths. Do not be wise in your own eyes; fear the LORD and depart from evil. It will be health to your flesh, and strength to your bones.

PROVERBS 3:5-8 NKJV

"So do not fear, for I am with you; do not be dismayed, for I am your God. I will strengthen you and help you; I will uphold you with my righteous right hand."

ISAIAH 41:10 NIV

As if expecting visitors, your cat is always up in the morning, looking well rested, washed, and groomed. At mealtimes, you never have to shout, "For the umpteenth time, will you come and eat?" Cats are fastidious about their litter boxes. They try to keep their claws filed down, and they never snore.

INGRID NEWKIRK

Your cat will never threaten your popularity by barking at three in the morning. He won't attack the mailman or eat the drapes, although he may climb the drapes to see how the room looks from the ceiling.

HELEN POWERS

I want to create a cat like the real cats I see crossing the streets, not like those you see in houses. They have nothing in common. The cat of the streets has bristling fur. It runs like a fiend, and if it looks at you, you think it is going to jump in your face.

PABLO PICASSO

Oh, catnip! What intoxicating appeal
Doth this herbaceous perennial impart!
In loving homes I chase
this madcap plant;
While families gather, laughing.
I love to raise a fuss.

WILLIAM SHAKESPAW

Simple Joys:
Contentment

And my God will meet all your needs according to the riches of his glory in Christ Jesus.

PHILIPPIANS 4:19 NIV

All the cats are happy, but Frick is an example of a very contented cat. Perhaps it is because of how he came to us that he seems to be so thankful for our home. The window well is no longer his bed, and he now receives regular veterinary attention. Food is always plentiful and he doesn't have to depend on what he can catch or wonder when he will eat his next meal. A warm house keeps him protected from the elements. Instead of always being on guard, he sits with paws folded under his body in deep contentment and trust of his circumstances.

Do we feel this much trust toward our heavenly Father? Are we willing to allow Him to provide for our needs, accepting His provision with gratitude and thankfulness? Sometimes, I am too independent in my thinking, believing I have to do everything myself. By letting go a little, and allowing God to bless me with His provision, I, too, can be contented.

Unlike us, cats never outgrow their delight in cat capacities, nor do they settle finally for limitations. Cats, I think, live out their lives fulfilling their expectations.

IRVING TOWNSEND

Everything that moves, serves to interest and amuse a cat. He is convinced that nature is busying herself with his diversion; he can conceive of no other purpose in the universe.

F. A. PARADIS DE MONCRIF

Surely the cat, when it assumes the meat loaf position and gazes meditatively through slitted eyes, is pondering thoughts of utter profundity.

MIJ COLSON BARNUM

Sunlight gently tickling the whiskers first thing this morning. A languid stroll around the premises. Nap. Toying with the chipmunk from the garden. Two kinds of fish for lunch. Nap. An awesome ball of yarn that somehow managed to fill three rooms. Catnip. (Actually, the catnip preceded the yarn.) Nap. A mouse or two, and that misfortunate bird. There was other stuff, too, but those are the highlights.

We tend to forget that happiness doesn't come as a result of getting something we don't have, but rather of recognizing and appreciating what we do have.

FREDERICK KEONIG

The lions may grow weak and hungry, but
those who seek the Lord lack no good thing.

PSALM 34:10 NIV

And my God shall supply all
your need according to His riches
in glory by Christ Jesus.

PHILIPPIANS 4:19 NKJV

As for the rich in this world, charge them
not to be proud and arrogant and
contemptuous of others, nor to set their
hopes on uncertain riches, but on God,
Who richly and ceaselessly provides us
with everything for [our] enjoyment.

1 TIMOTHY 6:17 AMP

He gives food to those who fear him;
he always remembers his covenant.

PSALM 111:5 NLT

The great charm of cats is their rampant egotism, their devil-may-care attitude toward responsibility, their disinclination to earn an honest dollar. In a continent which screams neurotically about cooperation and the Golden Rule, cats are disdainful of everything but their own immediate interests and they contrive to be so suave and delightful about it that they even receive the apotheosis of a National Cat Week.

ROBERTSON DAVIE

Everything I know I learned from my cat:
When you're hungry, eat. When you're tired,
nap in a sunbeam. When you go to the vet's,
pee on your owner.

GARY SMITH

Once I was young, and now I am old.
Yet I have never seen the godly abandoned
or their children begging for bread.

PSALM 37:25 NLT

Do what the LORD wants, and he
will give you your heart's desire.

PSALM 37:4 CEV

"Acknowledge the God of your father,
and serve him with wholehearted devotion
and with a willing mind, for the LORD searches
every heart and understands every desire
and every thought. If you seek him, he will
be found by you; but if you forsake him,
he will reject you forever."

1 CHRONICLES 28:9 NIV

The kitten has a luxurious, Bohemian, unpuritanical nature. It eats six meals a day, plays furiously with a toy mouse and a piece of rope, and suddenly falls into a deep sleep whenever the fit takes it. It never feels the necessity to do anything to justify its existence; it does not want to be a Good Citizen; it has never heard of Service. It knows that it is beautiful and delightful, and it considers that a sufficient contribution to the general good. And in return for its beauty and charm it expects fish, meat, and vegetables, a comfortable bed, a chair by the grate fire, and endless petting.

ROBERTSON DAVIES

Are cats lazy? Well, more power to them if they are. Which one of us has not entertained the dream of doing just as he likes, when and how he likes, and as much as he likes?

DR. FERNAND MERY

I saw the most beautiful cat today. It was sitting by the side of the road, its two front feet neatly and graciously together. Then it gravely swished around its tail to completely and snugly encircle itself. It was so fit and beautifully neat, that gesture, and so self-satisfied—so complacent.

ANNE MORROW LINDBERGH

"Therefore I tell you, do not worry about your life, what you will eat or drink; or about your body, what you will wear. Is not life more than food, and the body more than clothes? Look at the birds of the air; they do not sow or reap or store away in barns, and yet your heavenly Father feeds them. Are you not much more valuable than they? Can any one of you by worrying add a single hour to your life?"

MATTHEW 6:25–27 NIV

A cat isn't fussy—just so long as you remember he likes his milk in the shallow, rose-patterned saucer and his fish on the blue plate. From which he will take it, and eat it off the floor.

ARTHUR BRIDGES

The typical feline sleeps approximately sixteen hours a day, which means it spends about 60 percent of its life off-line. . . . Even in deepest slumber, a cat is still alert to its environment. The ears of a sleeping cat may twitch in response to sounds, and the slightest movement will instantly wake it.

DAVID BRUNNER AND SAM STALL

Good heavens, of what uncostly material
is our earthly happiness composed—
if we only knew it! What incomes have
we not had from a flower, and how
unfailing are the dividends of the seasons!

JAMES RUSSELL LOWELL

To live content with small means; to seek
elegance rather than luxury, and refinement
rather than fashion; to be worthy, not
respectable, and wealthy, not rich; to listen
to stars and birds, babes and sages, with
open heart; to study hard; to think quietly,
act frankly, talk gently, await occasions, hurry
never; in a word, to let the spiritual, unbidden
and unconscious, grow up through the
common—this is my symphony.

WILLIAM HENRY CHANNING

The best things in life are nearest: Breath
in your nostrils, light in your eyes, flowers at
your feet, duties at your hand, the path of
right just before you. Then do not grasp at
the stars, but do life's plain, common work
as it comes, certain that daily duties and daily
bread are the sweetest things in life.

ROBERT LOUIS STEVENSON

"But seek first his kingdom and his righteousness, and all these things will be given to you as well."

MATTHEW 6:33 NIV

And you also were included in Christ when you heard the message of truth, the gospel of your salvation. When you believed, you were marked in him with a seal, the promised Holy Spirit, who is a deposit guaranteeing our inheritance until the redemption of those who are God's possession—to the praise of his glory.

EPHESIANS 1:13–14 NIV

Give your burdens to the LORD, and he will take care of you. He will not permit the godly to slip and fall.

PSALM 55:22 NLT

You can't force simplicity; but you can invite it in by finding as much richness as possible in the few things at hand. Simplicity doesn't mean meagerness but rather a certain kind of richness, the fullness that appears when we stop stuffing the world with things.

THOMAS MOORE

He blinks upon the hearth-rug,
And yawns in deep content,
Accepting all the comforts
That Providence has sent. . .

Life will go on forever,
With all that cat can wish;
Warmth, and the glad procession
Of fish and milk and fish.

Only—the thought disturbs him—
He's noticed once or twice,
That times are somehow breeding
A nimbler race of mice.

SIR ALEXANDER GRAY

Good Things Come
to Those Who Wait:
Patience

*Be still before the L*ORD *and wait patiently for him; do not fret when people succeed in their ways, when they carry out their wicked schemes.*

PSALM 37:7 NIV

Admittedly, I am sometimes an impatient person. In this demanding and instantaneous society that I live in, I don't always wait patiently. Especially when it comes to situations where I think I've been wronged. I don't want to suffer. I want justice and I want it now!

Sometimes it seems that a cat's sole purpose in life is to remain as still as a rock and wait for unsuspecting prey to come along. They are patient, relaxed, and can wait without flinching until they pounce on their target. What if I were that willing to submit to God's plan? Can I be that still and patient to wait for God to act? That takes a great deal of trust in Him—the God who says He has a good plan for me, a plan that won't harm me but will prosper me. Lord, please grant me the patience to trust wholly in Your ways!

Cats are the natural companions of intellectuals. They are silent watchers of dreams, inspiration and patient research.

DR. FERNAND MERY

A cat can maintain a position of curled up somnolence on your knee until you are nearly upright. To the last minute she hopes your conscience will get the better of you and you will settle down again.

PAM BROWN

As anyone who has ever been around a cat for any length of time well knows, cats have enormous patience with the limitations of the human mind.

CLEVELAND AMORY

49

*And a servant of the Lord must not quarrel
but be gentle to all, able to teach, patient.*

2 Timothy 2:24 nkjv

*Be still in the presence of the Lord, and wait
patiently for him to act. Don't worry about evil
people who prosper or fret about their wicked
schemes. Stop being angry! Turn from your rage!
Do not lose your temper—it only leads to harm.
For the wicked will be destroyed, but those who
trust in the Lord will possess the land.*

Psalm 37:7–9 nlt

*Because you know that the testing of your
faith produces perseverance. Let perseverance
finish its work so that you may be mature
and complete, not lacking anything.*

James 1:3–4 niv

When my cats aren't happy, I'm not happy.
Not because I care about their mood but
because I know they're just sitting there
thinking up ways to get even.

PERCY BYSSHE SHELLEY

If animals could speak, the dog would
be a blundering outspoken fellow;
but the cat would have the rare grace
of never saying a word too much.

MARK TWAIN

"But the ones that fell on the good ground are those who, having heard the word with a noble and good heart, keep it and bear fruit with patience."

LUKE 8:15 NKJV

For whatever things were written before were written for our learning, that we through the patience and comfort of the Scriptures might have hope. Now may the God of patience and comfort grant you to be like-minded toward one another, according to Christ Jesus.

ROMANS 15:4–5 NKJV

May the Lord lead your hearts into a full understanding and expression of the love of God and the patient endurance that comes from Christ.

2 THESSALONIANS 3:5 NLT

53

Gentle eyes that see so much,
Paws that have the quiet touch,
Purrs to signal "all is well"
And show more love than words could tell.
Graceful movements touched with pride,
A calming presence by our side.
A friendship that takes time to grow—
Small wonder why we love them so.

UNKNOWN

I think one reason we admire cats, those of us who do, is their proficiency in one-upmanship. They always seem to come out on top, no matter what they are doing—or pretend they do. Rarely do you see a cat discomfited. They have no conscience, and they never regret. Maybe we secretly envy them.

BARBARA WEBSTER

The more we express our gratitude to God for our blessings, the more he will bring to our mind other blessings. The more we are aware of to be grateful for, the happier we become.

EZRA TAFT BENSON

Therefore, since we are surrounded by such a great cloud of witnesses, let us throw off everything that hinders and the sin that so easily entangles. And let us run with perseverance the race marked out for us.

HEBREWS 12:1 NIV

That you do not become sluggish, but imitate those who through faith and patience inherit the promises.

HEBREWS 6:12 NKJV

Of course, you get no credit for being patient if you are beaten for doing wrong. But if you suffer for doing good and endure it patiently, God is pleased with you.

1 PETER 2:20 NLT

The point in life is to know what's enough—
why envy those otherworld immortals?
With the happiness held in one inch-square
heart you can fill the whole space between
heaven and earth.

GENSEI

True happiness is of a retired nature, and an
enemy to pomp and noise; it arises, in the first
place, from the enjoyment of oneself, and in
the next from the friendship and conversation
of a few select companions.

JOSEPH ADDISON

A Poet's Cat, sedate and grave
As poet well could wish to have,
Was much addicted to inquire
For nooks to which she might retire,
And where, secure as mouse in chink,
She might repose, or sit and think.

WILLIAM COWPER

If there was any petting to be done, however, he chose to do it. Often he would sit looking at me, and then, moved by a delicate affection, come and pull at my coat and sleeve until he could touch my face with his nose, and then go away contented.

Charles Dudley Warner

We spend most of our time and energy in a kind of horizontal thinking. We move along the surface of things [but] there are times when we stop. We sit still. We lose ourselves in a pile of leaves or its memory. We listen and breezes from a whole other world begin to whisper.

James Carroll

*To those who by persistence in doing good
seek glory, honor and immortality,
he will give eternal life.*

ROMANS 2:7 NIV

*These trials will show that your faith is
genuine. It is being tested as fire tests
and purifies gold—though your faith is far
more precious than mere gold. So when
your faith remains strong through many trials,
it will bring you much praise and glory and
honor on the day when Jesus Christ is
revealed to the whole world.*

1 PETER 1:7 NLT

*Though he fall, he shall not be utterly cast
down; for the LORD upholds him with His hand.*

PSALM 37:24 NKJV

Frugality is one of the most beautiful and joyful words in the English language, and yet one that we are culturally cut off from understanding and enjoying. The consumption society has made us feel that happiness lies in having things, and has failed to teach us the happiness of not having things.

ELISE BOULDING

Happy people roll with the punches. They know from experience that everything changes. Today's good fortune may vanish tomorrow; today's crises may turn out to be tomorrow's good fortune. It's always better to wait and see before you decide the story has been written.

UNKNOWN

Oh loving puss, come hither and purr
Let me stroke your soft, warm fur.
Let me gaze into your loving eyes
How great their depth. . .how very wise.

What comfort your dear presence brings
I forget all sad, unhappy things.
Let no man live without this peace
Proof that God's wonders never cease.

DUTCH CARRIE

The Art of
Being Quiet

He says, "Be still, and know that I am God; I will be exalted among the nations, I will be exalted in the earth."

P SALM 46:10 NIV

Have you seen the cats?" is a question I hear often. I check several places, including our three bedrooms. A favorite hangout is the top of a short bookcase, right next to a sunny window in the office. Sometimes the cats sleep there, but most often, this is their quiet place. Warmed by the sun with a view of the yard, the cats have learned to just "be" in this place. To be still, relax—maybe even reflecting on all that is going on in their world.

I am not very good at being quiet. I am always busy. Too busy, oftentimes, to take in the beauty that is God's creation. My cats teach me to take time to be quiet and to bask in being still—to stop my hands from work and fully feel the presence of God and His Word for me. And. . .perhaps. . .to sit by that sunny window for a few minutes.

When my cat lies down,
it is with utmost gravity.

No circular trampling first
like a clumsy canine,
no great sigh
like a human
being on a couch.

My cat lies down slowly,
naturally, smoothly,
participating with
controlled abandon
in a dignified
gravitational event.

ALAN HARRIS

There's no need for a piece of sculpture
in a home that has a cat.

WESLEY BATES

Cats MUST have comfy places to sit and look
out. To the dedicated bird-watcher, nothing
makes the time pass quicker, and the whiskers
twitch faster, than the object of her natural,
abiding interest and careful study.

INGRID NEWKIRK

*Pay attention to advice and accept
correction, so you can live sensibly.*

PROVERBS 19:20 CEV

*"But all this was done that the Scriptures
of the prophets might be fulfilled."*

MATTHEW 26:56 NKJV

*Everything God says is true—and it's a
shield for all who come to him for safety.*

PROVERBS 30:5 CEV

*I have hidden your word in my heart
that I might not sin against you.*

PSALM 119:11 NIV

Cats are rather delicate creatures
and they are subject to a good many
ailments, but I never heard of one
who suffered from insomnia.

JOSEPH WOOD KRUTCH

He seems the incarnation of everything
soft and silky and velvety, without a sharp
edge in his composition, a dreamer whose
philosophy is sleep and let sleep.

SAKI

I have learned a lot from my cat.
When life is loud and scary, go under
the bed and nap. When you want someone
to notice you, sit on the book that person is
reading. And if someone sits in your chair,
glare at her until she moves.

CAROL SMITH

*I want you to recall the words spoken
in the past by the holy prophets and the
command given by our Lord and Savior
through your apostles.*

2 PETER 3:2 NIV

*Long ago in many ways and at many times
God's prophets spoke his message to our
ancestors. But now at last, God sent his Son
to bring his message to us. God created
the universe by his Son, and everything
will someday belong to the Son.*

HEBREWS 1:1–2 CEV

*Your word is a lamp for my feet,
a light on my path.*

PSALM 119:105 NIV

The sun slants in, its light a wedge
Of carpet by the door.
And to that slice of sunlight
Goes my cat, now, to restore
Herself. This nap is therapeutic
(Like the tuna she devoured).
She seems to need this daily bask.
She thinks she's solar powered.

LEE ANNY WYNN SNOOK

Slow down and enjoy life. It's not only the scenery you miss by going too fast—you also miss the sense of where you are going and why.

EDDIE CANTOR

The cat lives alone, has no need of society, obeys only when she pleases, pretends to sleep that she may see more clearly, and scratches everything on which she can lay her paw.

FRANÇOIS R. CHATEAUBRIAND

When your words came, I ate them; they were my joy and my heart's delight, for I bear your name, LORD God Almighty.

JEREMIAH 15:16 NIV

For the word of God is alive and powerful. It is sharper than the sharpest two-edged sword, cutting between soul and spirit, between joint and marrow. It exposes our innermost thoughts and desires.

HEBREWS 4:12 NLT

Like newborn babies you should crave (thirst for, earnestly desire) the pure (unadulterated) spiritual milk, that by it you may be nurtured and grow unto [completed] salvation.

1 PETER 2:2 AMP

I think I could turn and live with animals,
they are so placid and self-contained,
I stand and look at them long and long.

WALT WHITMAN

A sleeping cat in a room has the effect of
nothing short of a lit candle. It is a carrier
of peace, an agent of quiet. And should that
cat stretch full-length from paw to tail,
its influence is only heightened.

CAROL SMITH

When I dance, I dance; when I sleep,
I sleep. Nay, when I walk alone in a beautiful
orchard, if my thoughts are some part of
the time taken up with foreign occurrences,
I some part of the time call them back again
to my walk, to the orchard, to the sweetness
of the solitude, and to myself.

MICHEL DE MONTAIGNE

If a dog jumps up into your lap, it is because
he is fond of you; but if a cat does the same
thing, it is because your lap is warmer.

ALFRED NORTH WHITEHEAD

No catnip tree
Could offer bliss
Of magnitude
To equal this
As in a transport
Of delight
My spaced-out cougar
Spends the night
His nose in cozy
Rendezvous
With my malodorous
Jogging shoe.

DOROTHY HELLER

My heart has heard you say,
"Come and talk with me." And my
heart responds, "LORD, I am coming."

PSALM 27:8 NLT

Therefore you shall lay up these My words in
your [minds and] hearts and in your [entire]
being, and bind them for a sign upon your
hands and as forehead bands between your
eyes. And you shall teach them to your
children, speaking of them when you sit in
your house and when you walk along the road,
when you lie down and when you rise up.

DEUTERONOMY 11:18–19 AMP

Seek the LORD while He may be found,
call upon Him while He is near.

ISAIAH 55:6 NKJV

If by chance I seated myself to write, she very slyly, very tenderly, seeking protection and caresses, would softly take her place on my knee and follow the comings and goings of my pen—sometimes effacing, with an unintentional stroke of her paw, lines of whose tenor she disapproved.

PIERRE LOTI

All cats and kittens, whether royal Persians or of the lowliest estate, resent patronage, jocoseness (which they rightly hold to be in bad taste), and demonstrative affection,—those lavish embraces which lack delicacy and reserve.

AGNES REPPLIER

[Our cat] is ever close, ever present, ever observing but she rarely intrudes. Her world is linked to ours but does not revolve around it. To share your life with a cat is to see grace of body and spirit on a daily basis, if you pay attention, if you know what to look for.

BRIAN KILCOMMONS AND SARA WILSON

Cleanliness Is
Next to Godliness

Do you not know that your bodies are temples of the Holy Spirit, who is in you, whom you have received from God? You are not your own; you were bought at a price. Therefore honor God with your bodies.

1 Corinthians 6:19–20 niv

A cat's sense of smell is fourteen times more powerful than humans'. Most predators, including cats, track by smell. Feral cats, especially, will spend what seems to be an inordinate amount of time grooming themselves. What they are doing, however, is removing any evidence of food or other scent that may identify them to a potential predator. Grooming also rids the coat of dirt and parasites, such as fleas. And because cats don't have sweat glands, grooming aids in making them feel cooler on hot days.

Do we take care of our bodies as well as our cats? I know I don't. I sometimes take the gift of my body for granted, especially when it comes to eating healthy foods or getting enough exercise or rest. Next time I see Frick, Yoda, or Chewy grooming themselves, I will recommit to taking better care of the gift that God gave me—my body!

I know I was designed to be
Adored by all who encounter me
With glossy fur and emerald eyes
My glory's sure to mesmerize
Those hapless humans who think that
A dog's a dog; a cat's a cat
Will surely come around to see
The miracle that is me.

FRANNY SYUFY

I don't think it is so much the actual bath that most cats dislike; I think it's the fact that they have to spend a good part of the day putting their hair back in place.

DEBBIE PETERSON

Just as the would-be debutante will fret and fuss over every detail till all is perfect, so will the fastidious feline patiently toil until every whisker tip is in place.

LYNN HOLLYN

It would be hard indeed to list all the fascinating qualities attributed to cats over the ages—especially since every cat seems to have a unique temperament. Nevertheless, most cats share a few common characteristics. . .dignity, complexity, empathy, grace, presence, cleanliness, and charm.

ERIC SWANSON

Don't copy the behavior and customs of this world, but let God transform you into a new person by changing the way you think. Then you will learn to know God's will for you, which is good and pleasing and perfect.

ROMANS 12:2 NLT

Who is smart enough to explain everything? Wisdom makes you cheerful and gives you a smile.

ECCLESIASTES 8:1 CEV

"The LORD doesn't see things the way you see them. People judge by outward appearance, but the LORD looks at the heart."

1 SAMUEL 16:7 NLT

I simply can't resist a cat, particularly a purring one. They are the cleanest, cunningest, and most intelligent things I know, outside of the girl you love, of course.

MARK TWAIN

A cat licking herself solves most of the problems of infection. We wash too much and finally it kills us.

WILLIAM CARLOS WILLIAMS

A kitten is the most irresistible comedian in the world. Its wide-open eyes gleam with wonder and mirth. It darts madly at nothing at all, and then, as though suddenly checked in the pursuit, prances sideways on its hind legs with ridiculous agility and zeal.

AGNES REPPLIER

*Be honest in your judgment and do not
decide at a glance (superficially and by
appearances); but judge fairly and righteously.*

JOHN 7:24 AMP

*Your beauty should not come from outward
adornment, such as elaborate hairstyles and
the wearing of gold jewelry or fine clothes.
Rather, it should be that of your inner self, the
unfading beauty of a gentle and quiet spirit,
which is of great worth in God's sight. For this
is the way the holy women of the past who put
their hope in God used to adorn themselves.*

1 PETER 3:3–5 NIV

The cat is surprisingly similar to other
high-tech devices you may already own.
Like personal digital assistants, it is compact
and portable. Like a home security system,
it is capable of functioning autonomously
for extended periods without direct human
intervention. But unlike virtually any other
product. . .it is, for the most part, self-cleaning.

DAVID BRUNNER AND SAM STALL

It is easy to understand why the rabble dislike cats. A cat is beautiful; it suggests ideas of luxury, cleanliness, voluptuous pleasures.

CHARLES BAUDELAIRE

There is the little matter of disposal of droppings in which the cat is far ahead of its rivals. The dog is somehow thrilled by what he or any of his friends have produced, hates to leave it, adores smelling it, and sometimes eats it. . . . The cat covers it up if he can.

PAUL GALLICO

"Yes, just as you can identify a tree by its fruit, so you can identify people by their actions."

MATTHEW 7:20 NLT

So God created man in His own image, in the image and likeness of God He created him; male and female He created them.

GENESIS 1:27 AMP

You, LORD, are our Father. We are nothing but clay, but you are the potter who molded us.

ISAIAH 64:8 CEV

Let love be your highest goal! But you should also desire the special abilities the Spirit gives.

1 CORINTHIANS 14:1 NLT

Now a cat will not take an excursion merely because a man wants a walking companion. Walking is a human habit into which dogs readily fall but it is a distasteful form of exercise to a cat unless he has a purpose in view.

CARL VAN VECHTEN

I shall never forget the indulgence with which Dr. Johnson treated Hodge, his cat, for whom he himself used to go out and buy oysters, lest the servants, having that trouble, should take a dislike to the poor creature.

JAMES BOSWELL

It was [my cat's] firm belief that I had the power to turn off the rain, brush away the clouds, make the sun come back to shine upon the window ledge, modify the temperature, (and) perform other miracles as required. I found my failure to live up to his high esteem somewhat embarrassing.

ERA ZISTEL

The cat has been described as the most perfect animal, the acme of muscular perfection and the supreme example in the animal kingdom of the coordination of mind and muscle.

ROSEANNE AMBROSE BROWN

Finally, brethren, whatever things are true, whatever things are noble, whatever things are just, whatever things are pure, whatever things are lovely, whatever things are of good report, if there is any virtue and if there is anything praiseworthy—meditate on these things.

PHILIPPIANS 4:8 NKJV

For we are God's masterpiece. He has created us anew in Christ Jesus, so we can do the good things he planned for us long ago.

EPHESIANS 2:10 NLT

The LORD will guide you always; he will satisfy your needs in a sun-scorched land and will strengthen your frame. You will be like a well-watered garden, like a spring whose waters never fail.

ISAIAH 58:11 NIV

I am the cat of cats. I am
The everlasting cat!
Cunning and old, and sleek as jam,
The everlasting cat!
I hunt the vermin in the night—
The everlasting cat!
For I see best without the light—
The everlasting cat!

WILLIAM BRIGHTY RANDS

Is it yet another survival of jungle
instinct, this hiding away from
prying eyes at important times?
Or merely a gesture of independence,
a challenge to man and his stupid ways?

MICHAEL JOSEPH

More than likely it was the cat who
first coined and put into practice the
sage advice: "If you would have a thing
done well, you must do it yourself."

LAWRENCE N. JOHNSON

Unconditional
Love

Whoever does not love does not know God, because God is love.

1 John 4:8 niv

Our cat named Frick lived in the window well when we bought our home, so he "came" with the purchase. It took over a year of soft conversation, food, and careful touching before he'd consent to come into the house. About a year after Frick's conversion, another of our feral-turned-house cats gave birth to the litter that included Yoda and Chewbacca. These cats had the benefit of knowing human companions early on, so their entry into our home was much less difficult.

However, that first winter with all of them in the house consisted of a lot of back arching, hissing, and scratching. Things have settled down substantially since our furry children came to live with us, but the whole situation made me consider what God asks of us—to put aside differences to love one another unconditionally. When we value another over ourselves, we please our Father.

Humans: No fur, no paws, no tail.
They run away from mice. They never
get enough sleep. How can you help
but love such an absurd animal?

AN ANONYMOUS CAT ON HOMO SAPIENS

Four little Persians, but only one looked in my
direction. I extended a tentative finger and two
soft paws clung to it. There was a contented
sound of purring, I suspect on both our parts.

GEORGE FREEDLEY

If you have a cat, congratulations. You have a relationship in which you are unconditionally loved, endlessly forgiven for your mistakes, never judged, and constantly entertained. A cat can make the stresses of your day disappear just by curling up in your lap at night.

PAM JOHNSON-BENNETT

The reasons we share our lives with our cats may be different, and yet somehow they are tied by a common thread. It is love that links us together: love of the animals and their love for us, for reasons known only to them, but it's all the same. It's all love.

SARA WILSON

I gave my cat a bath once. I thought she'd feel so much better. But in the end, we were both the worse for it and I've never done it to either of us since. Though I have to admit that every so often we find ourselves in the bathroom at the same time, and I feel sure we both remember the horror.

CAROL SMITH

God stays one with everyone who openly says that Jesus is the Son of God. That's how we stay one with God and are sure that God loves us. God is love. If we keep on loving others, we will stay one in our hearts with God, and he will stay one with us.

1 JOHN 4:15–16 CEV

This is real love—not that we loved God, but that he loved us and sent his Son as a sacrifice to take away our sins.

1 JOHN 4:10 NLT

Think how much the Father loves us. He loves us so much that he lets us be called his children, as we truly are.

1 JOHN 3:1 CEV

James Herriot, the beloved veterinarian, enjoyed the company of cats from the time he was a small boy. He stated, "Their innate grace and daintiness and their deeply responsive affection made them all dear to me. . . . I have felt cats rubbing their faces against mine and touching my cheek with claws carefully sheathed. These things, to me, are expressions of love."

The more one does and sees and feels, the more one is able to do, and the more genuine may be one's appreciation of fundamental things like home, and love, and understanding companionship.

AMELIA EARHART

Guard well within yourself that treasure, kindness. Know how to give without hesitation, how to lose without regret, how to acquire without meanness.

GEORGE SAND

Personally, I would not give a fig for any man's religion whose horse, cat, and dog do not feel its benefits. Life in any form is our perpetual responsibility.

S. PARKES CADMAN

*"I will heal their waywardness and
love them freely, for my anger
has turned away from them."*

HOSEA 14:4 NIV

*That is what the Scriptures mean when
they say, "No eye has seen, no ear has heard,
and no mind has imagined what God has
prepared for those who love him."*

1 CORINIHIANS 2:9 NLT

*And hope does not put us to shame,
because God's love has been poured
out into our hearts through the Holy
Spirit, who has been given to us.*

ROMANS 5:5 NIV

If the pull of the outside world is strong, there is also a pull toward the human. The cat may disappear on its own errands, but sooner or later, it returns once again for a little while, to greet us with its own type of love.

LLOYD ALEXANDER

The birth of a kitten is one of the most moving events you can see. New life offers an opportunity to enjoy innocence, trust, and love generously given.

MORDECAI SIEGAL

If having a soul means being able to feel
love and loyalty and gratitude, then animals
are better off than a lot of humans.

JAMES HERRIOT

For I am persuaded beyond doubt (am sure) that neither death nor life, nor angels nor principalities, nor things impending and threatening nor things to come, nor powers, nor height nor depth, nor anything else in all creation will be able to separate us from the love of God which is in Christ Jesus our Lord.

Romans 8:38–39 amp

Friendship is the hardest thing in the world to explain. It's not something you learn in school. But if you haven't learned the meaning of friendship, you really haven't learned anything.

Muhammad Ali

Until one has loved an animal, a part of one's soul remains unawakened.

Anatole France

The glory of friendship is not the outstretched hand, nor the kindly smile, nor the joy of companionship; it's the spiritual inspiration that comes to one when he discovers that someone else believes in him and is willing to trust him with his friendship.

Ralph Waldo Emerson

There isn't much better in this life than finding a way to spend a few hours in conversation with people you respect and love. You have to carve this time out of your life, because you aren't really living without it.

Unknown

To anyone who has ever been owned by a cat, it will come as no surprise that there are all sorts of things about your cat you will never, as long as you live, forget. Not the least of these is your first sight of him or her.

CLEVELAND AMORY

Even the shiest cat craves her owner's affection. While you're busy typing away or engrossed in a video, she may just crawl out from her hiding place under the bed and touch her nose to your bare foot or rub her whiskers against your shin— just to make sure you're there.

ERIC SWANSON

We have confidence in the Lord that you are doing and will continue to do the things we command. May the Lord direct your hearts into God's love and Christ's perseverance.

2 Thessalonians 3:4–5 niv

"For the Lord your God is living among you. He is a mighty savior. He will take delight in you with gladness. With his love, he will calm all your fears. He will rejoice over you with joyful songs."

Zephaniah 3:17 nlt

Examine me, O Lord, and prove me; test my heart and my mind. For Your loving-kindness is before my eyes, and I have walked in Your truth [faithfully].

Psalm 26:2–3 amp

When your cat rubs the side of its face along your leg, it's affectionately marking you with its scent, identifying you as its private property, saying, in effect, "You belong to me."

SUSAN McDONOUGH, DMV

What greater gift than the love of a cat?

CHARLES DICKENS

Among those whom I like or admire,
I can find no common denominator,
but among those whom I love, I can:
all of them make me laugh.

W. H. AUDEN

It is impossible for a lover of cats
to banish these alert, gentle,
and discriminating little friends,
who give us just enough of their
regard and complaisance to
make us hunger for more.

AGNES REPPLIER

Sharing
the Labor

Two are better than one, because they have a good return for their labor.

Ecclesiastes 4:9 niv

I've learned that most people think that cats are natural hunters. The truth is that the ability to hunt for food is taught by the kittens' mother. Fortunately for Frick, Yoda, and Chewy, their mothers taught them well and they are all three excellent mousers.

Cats are usually solitary hunters, which was why I was so amazed at the several times I have seen all three of mine hunting collaboratively. One cat will circle around the back, while another keeps watch and the third is crouched and ready to move in. They work together like a well oiled machine, reading one another's body language and instinctively knowing what to do next.

Just as the cats found, combining our energies and talents makes us both more efficient and likely to succeed. There is help in times when difficulties emerge, and companionship during the good times. I know I have more fun when I work alongside others, and as the old adage says, "many hands make light work."

My soul mate was Captain. Together we caught frogs, climbed trees, hid from my brothers— we were a team. No one had ever told us the lie that cats are aloof, independent, or uncaring. Captain certainly never was. He comforted me when I was lonely; I cuddled him when he was. He was an incorruptibly fine soul, and I am the richer to have known him.

SARA WILSON

We can feel lonely with lots of others around. We may feel "not okay." It is easy to give up hope. We need to hear a voice that says, "I choose you." And the touch of a finger— or a paw—means so much.

MARTA FELBER

You remember my ideal cat has always a huge rat in its mouth, just going out of sight—though going out of sight in itself has a peculiar pleasure.

EMILY DICKINSON

He came into my life with eyes so blue
I named him Frank, for Frank Sinatra.
Those eyes saw me through a move,
and the loss of a love, and the refinding
of myself. And I buried him with daisies
and was so grateful that I had been his.

And He said to them, "Which of you shall have a friend, and go to him at midnight and say to him, 'Friend, lend me three loaves; for a friend of mine has come to me on his journey, and I have nothing to set before him'; and he will answer from within and say, 'Do not trouble me; the door is now shut, and my children are with me in bed; I cannot rise and give to you'? I say to you, though he will not rise and give to him because he is his friend, yet because of his persistence he will rise and give him as many as he needs."

LUKE 11:5–8 NKJV

Like annoying women who marry a man and then instantly want to reform him, cats have very firm ideas about what they want in a lifetime companion. . . . After all, they didn't choose you, they got stuck with you. Like mail-order brides, if they had hissed and spat and refused to be carried over the threshold, who knows what would have become of them?

INGRID NEWKIRK

When I play with my cat, who knows if I am not a pastime to her more than she is to me? . . . Who knows but that she pities me for being no wiser than to play with her; and laughs, and censures my folly in making sport for her, when we two play together.

MICHEL DE MONTAIGNE

Many a person has held close, throughout their entire lives, two friends that always remained strange to one another, because one of them attracted by virtue of similarity, the other by difference.

EMIL LUDWIG

Don't walk behind me; I may not lead
Don't walk in front of me; I may not follow.
Just walk beside me and be my friend.

UNKNOWN

*As iron sharpens iron,
so one person sharpens another.*

PROVERBS 27:17 NIV

*Two people are better off than one, for
they can help each other succeed. If
one person falls, the other can reach out
and help. But someone who falls alone is
in real trouble. Likewise, two people lying
close together can keep each other warm.
But how can one be warm alone?*

ECCLESIASTES 4:9–11 NLT

*And my God shall supply all
your need according to His
riches in glory by Christ Jesus.*

PHILIPPIANS 4:19 NKJV

In the sweetness of friendship; let there
be laughter and sharing of pleasures.
For in the dew of little things the heart
finds its morning and is refreshed.

KAHLIL GIBRAN

There is something about the presence
of a cat. . .that seems to take the
bite out of being alone.

LOUIS J. CAMUTI

I'd like to think I owned the cat,
that condescends to share my flat,
I give him all of my rationed food,
and cater to his every mood,
I'd like to think he'd go to seed,
if I weren't there to meet his every need,
And yet the fact is plain to see,
That dogggone cat, owns me!

VANESSA ROGERSON

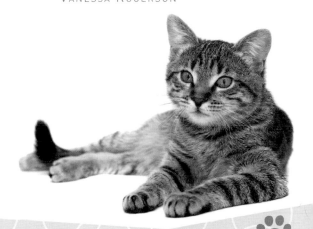

When we honestly ask ourselves which person in our lives means the most to us, we often find that it is those who, instead of giving advice, solutions, or cures, have chosen rather to share our pain and touch our wounds with a warm and tender hand.

HENRI NOUWEN

For I am convinced that neither death nor life, neither angels nor demons, neither the present nor the future, nor any powers, neither height nor depth, nor anything else in all creation, will be able to separate us from the love of God that is in Christ Jesus our Lord.

ROMANS 8:38–40 NIV

"I will praise you, LORD. Although you were angry with me, your anger has turned away and you have comforted me."

ISAIAH 12:1 NIV

I will turn their mourning into gladness; I will give them comfort and joy instead of sorrow.

JEREMIAH 31:13 NIV

I rarely meddled in the cat's personal affairs and she rarely meddled in mine. Neither of us was foolish enough to attribute human emotions to our pets.

KINKY FRIEDMAN

Cats grace us with their affection. . . . When they curl up on your lap, it's because they think you're worth spending time with. When they climb onto your shoulder, it's because they trust that you will carry them safely. When they lie across your magazine, it's because they can't believe their best friend would rather look at this flat, boring thing than their sleek, gorgeous, purring selves.

BRIAN KILCOMMONS AND SARA WILSON

Before a cat will condescend
To treat you as a trusted friend,
Some little token of esteem
Is needed, like a dish of cream.

T. S. ELIOT

We suffer in the hope that you will be comforted and saved. And because we are comforted, you will also be comforted, as you patiently endure suffering like ours. You never disappoint us. You suffered as much as we did, and we know that you will be comforted as we were.

2 CORINTHIANS 1:6–7 CEV

And now, dear children, continue in him, so that when he appears we may be confident and unashamed before him at his coming.

1 JOHN 2:28 NIV

For you know that we dealt with each of you as a father deals with his own children, encouraging, comforting and urging you to live lives worthy of God, who calls you into his kingdom and glory.

1 THESSALONIANS 2:11–12 NIV

Peaches was a kitty who loved to chase squirrels. Therefore, her owners were shocked when a very pregnant Peaches adopted an abandoned baby squirrel. When she gave birth to her kittens, she placed the baby squirrel with her brood and nursed them together!

ALLAN ZULLO AND MARA BOVSUN

In many ways I behave toward my cats as if they were human—and I'm not alone in that. Similarly, to my cats I am some sort of cat. We are all a bit confused on the overlap between people and cats.

ROGER TABOR

The cat does not offer services.
The cat offers itself. Of course he wants
care and shelter. You don't buy love
for nothing. Like all pure creatures,
cats are practical.

WILLIAM S. BURROUGHS

Friendship is unnecessary, like
philosophy, like art, like the universe
itself (for God did not need to create).
It has no survival value; rather it is one of
those things which give value to survival.

C. S. LEWIS

Cats have intercepted my footsteps
at the ankle for so long that my gait,
both at home and on tour, has been
compared to that of a man wading
through low surf.

ROY BLOUNT JR.

Surveying the
Kingdom

Have confidence in your leaders and submit to their authority, because they keep watch over you as those who must give an account. Do this so that their work will be a joy, not a burden, for that would be of no benefit to you.

HEBREWS 13:17 NIV

Yoda likes to look out the window—and will sometimes sit there for hours at a time. Her eyes dart to and fro, looking at what may be in "her" yard. Sometimes her muscles will tense and I'll hear a low, guttural sound as she sees something that doesn't please her. While she could never defend us like a watchdog, her intent to defend her turf is no less sincere.

Matthew Henry says in his commentary on Hebrews 13:17 that we are to acknowledge that our spiritual leaders are not only there to teach and lead us in holiness, but to watch over everything that might be hurtful to our souls. They are to protect us by warning us of danger and Satan's tricks. This charge is of utmost importance. Loving, encouraging, and supporting our pastors and mentors in the building up of the Kingdom is a responsibility we should all take seriously.

137

A cat is a patient listener, even when you're telling a story for the third time. A cat is the most dependable alarm clock you'll ever have. A cat will show you how to enjoy life. A cat chooses the company he keeps.

PAM JOHNSON-BENNETT

In everyone's life, at some time, our inner fire goes out. It is then burst into flame by an encounter with another human being. We should all be thankful for those people who rekindle the inner spirit.

ALBERT SCHWEITZER

The popularizing of the cat by writers and artists such as Edward Lear and Beatrix Potter has made them endearing images for children's pets. Edward Lear was so devoted to his cat Foss that when he moved, his new villa was constructed exactly like his old house so as not to inconvenience his cat in any way!

ROGER TABOR

The sacrifice that honors me is a thankful heart. Obey me, and I, your God, will show my power to save.

PSALM 50:23 CEV

Jesus replied: " 'Love the Lord your God with all your heart and with all your soul and with all your mind.' This is the first and greatest commandment. And the second is like it: 'Love your neighbor as yourself.' All the Law and the Prophets hang on these two commandments."

MATTHEW 22:37–40 NIV

For everything comes from him and exists by his power and is intended for his glory. All glory to him forever! Amen.

ROMANS 11:36 NLT

We should be careful to get out of an experience only the wisdom that is in it— and stop there; lest we be like the cat that sits down on a hot stove lid. She will never sit down on a hot stove lid again— and that is well, but she will also never sit down on a cold one .

MARK TWAIN

Everything that is new or uncommon raises a pleasure in the imagination, because it fills the soul with an agreeable surprise, gratifies its curiosity, and gives it an idea of which it was not before possessed.

JOSEPH ADDISON

"If you remain in me and my words remain in you, ask whatever you wish, and it will be done for you. This is to my Father's glory, that you bear much fruit, showing yourselves to be my disciples."

JOHN 15:7-8 NIV

Not unto us, O LORD, not unto us, but to Your name give glory, because of Your mercy, because of Your truth.

PSALM 115:1 NKJV

Tell everyone of every nation, "Praise the glorious power of the LORD. He is wonderful! Praise him and bring an offering into his temple. Worship the LORD, majestic and holy."

1 CHRONICLES 16:28-29 CEV

143

In the human world, there is a thing called a "mistake." There's no exact translation in the feline language. . . . The concept is quite confusing to cats since everything we do is done both correctly and on purpose.

JOE GARDEN

It is a matter to gain the affection of a cat. He is a philosophical animal, tenacious of his own habits, fond of order and neatness, and disinclined to extravagant sentiment. He will be your friend, if he finds you worthy of friendship, but not your slave. He keeps his free will though he loves, and will not do for you what he thinks unreasonable; but if he once gives himself to you, it is with absolute confidence and fidelity of affection.

THEOPHILE GAUTIER

Cats, with their shining eyes and silent footfalls, have always eluded explanation. Throughout the several thousand years of shared history between cats and human beings, cats have been a source of wonder and unease, reverence and superstition.

STEPHEN BUDIANSKY

The dog is a pack animal. He hunts in a pack and his whole social structure is built on the pack mentality. A cat, on the other hand, is a sociable animal but not the pack animal that a dog is. His social structure is built upon his sense of territory.

PAM JOHNSON-BENNETT

Therefore, as God's chosen people, holy and dearly loved, clothe yourselves with compassion, kindness, humility, gentleness and patience. Bear with each other and forgive one another if any of you has a grievance against someone. Forgive as the Lord forgave you. And over all these virtues put on love, which binds them all together in perfect unity. Let the peace of Christ rule in your hearts, since as members of one body you were called to peace. And be thankful.

COLOSSIANS 3:12–15 NIV

The cat is the animal to whom the Creator gave the biggest eye, the softest fur, the most supremely delicate nostrils, a mobile ear, an unrivaled paw, a curved claw, borrowed from a rose tree.

COLETTE

The things which man gives to him are not so precious or essential that he will trade them for his birthright, which is the right to be himself—a furred four-footed being of ancient lineage, loving silence and aloneness and the night, and esteeming the smell of rat's blood above any possible human excellence.

ALAN DEVOE

You will find as you look back upon your life that the moments when you have truly lived are the moments when you have done things in the spirit of love.

HENRY DRUMMOND

A cat's got her own opinion of human beings. She don't say much, but you can tell enough to make you anxious not to hear the whole of it.

JEROME K. JEROME

Cats were brought into human society by
a deliberate act of adventuresome and
curious human beings; there they grew to
a critical mass in a culture that in time came
to venerate them en masse; thence they
spread wherever man went, a vine circling
the tree of humanity that always planted
its own roots nearby, yet apart.

STEPHEN BUDIANSKY

I never cease to be amazed by how incredibly
clever and manipulative the average pet
cat can be. It is rather humbling and
intensely amusing to think that we can be so
successfully trained by a small furry creature.
Cats are supposedly well beneath us on the
evolutionary scale, but sometimes I wonder.

VICKY HALLS

But as for you, O man of God, flee from all these things; aim at and pursue righteousness (right standing with God and true goodness), godliness (which is the loving fear of God and being Christlike), faith, love, steadfastness (patience), and gentleness of heart.

1 Timothy 6:11 amp

May God give you more and more grace and peace as you grow in your knowledge of God and Jesus our Lord. By his divine power, God has given us everything we need for living a godly life. We have received all of this by coming to know him, the one who called us to himself by means of his marvelous glory and excellence.

2 Peter 1:2–3 nlt

He's nothing much but fur
And two round eyes of blue,
He has a giant purr
And a midget mew.

He darts and pats the air,
He starts and cocks his ear,
When there is nothing there
For him to see and hear. . . .

Then halfway through a leap
His startled eyeballs close,
And he drops off to sleep
With one paw on his nose.

ELEANOR FARJEON

The beauty and fascination we find in cats are much the same as what we feel for the wildest things in nature, with the added fascination that these particular wild and beautiful things are willing to admit us to their world, even though they don't have any particular need to.

STEPHEN BUDIANSKY

Communication and understanding are the two most important links between cats and their owners. It is obvious to sensitive and caring owners that their cats are aware when the owners are unhappy or in ill health. Likewise, the cats respond with joyful play when the owner's mood is jolly.

ANITRA FRAZIER AND NORMA ECKROATE

Furry Fun

*A cheerful heart is good medicine,
but a crushed spirit dries up the bones.*

PROVERBS 17:22 NIV

The rattle of a ball as it rolls across the floor is followed by the thumpty-thump of an orange cat chasing after it. Frick then hops up on the coffee table and is mesmerized by how a writing pen twirls when he swats at it with his paw then follows it as it drops to the floor. He discovers that the pen doesn't twirl the same way as it did on the table. Chewy starts to chase his sister, Yoda, their sleek, black forms leaning into the curve as they round into the hallway. Both slide on the hardwood floors, which makes the chase that much more fun.

Our cats love to play! Just like their human counterparts, play is enjoyable and oftentimes involves imagination. It also helps to release pent-up energy and is good exercise. But, more than that, it makes us happy!

Our Father God knows we need to have times of play, to relax, smile, and be light-hearted. Having fun helps us balance life with work and other difficult activities, and brings us joy. Now, where's that ball?

If a man insisted always on being serious, and never allowed himself a bit of fun and relaxation, he would go mad or become unstable without knowing it.

HERODOTUS

I think my favorite thing in the house has to be the cat. . .mainly because she's just like a big piece of noisy Velcro when you toss her at the sofa.

MICHELLE ARGABRITE

It is impossible to keep a straight face
in the presence of one or more kittens.

CYNTHIA E. VARNADO

Eyes are indeed the window to the soul,
especially with cats. Cats, not being a
deceiving group, will let you know precisely
what they think of you with a glance.

BRIAN KILCOMMONS AND SARAH WILSON

The real joy of life is in its play. Play is
anything we do for the joy and love of doing
it, apart from any profit, compulsion, or
sense of duty. It is the real joy of living.

WALTER RAUSCHBUSCH

"I am coming to you now, but I say these things while I am still in the world, so that they may have the full measure of my joy within them."

JOHN 17:13 NIV

Is anyone among you in trouble? Let them pray. Is anyone happy? Let them sing songs of praise.

JAMES 5:13 NIV

For our heart shall rejoice in Him, because we have trusted in His holy name.

PSALM 33:21 NKJV

Singing psalms and hymns and spiritual songs among yourselves, and making music to the Lord in your hearts.

EPHESIANS 5:19 NLT

I have noticed that what cats most appreciate in a human being is not the ability to produce food, which they take for granted—but his or her entertainment value.

GEOFFREY HOUSEHOLD

I woke up this morning to the sound of two cats entwined in a roly-poly play fight making their snowball way down the hall until they separated only to chase each other back around and start all over again. And I have to admit, I wished I could be a part of the gymnastics.

CAROL SMITH

Seize the moment of excited curiosity on any subject to solve your doubts; for if you let it pass, the desire may never return, and you may remain in ignorance.

WILLIAM WIRT

A kitten is so flexible that she is almost double; the hind parts are equivalent to another kitten with which the forepart plays. She does not discover that her tail belongs to her until you tread on it.

HENRY DAVID THOREAU

So now we can rejoice in our wonderful new relationship with God because our Lord Jesus Christ has made us friends of God.

ROMANS 5:11 NLT

The LORD is my strength and my shield; my heart trusted in Him, and I am helped; therefore my heart greatly rejoices, and with my song I will praise Him.

PSALM 28:7 NKJV

"Until now you have not asked for anything in my name. Ask and you will receive, and your joy will be complete."

JOHN 16:24 NIV

Happiness is like a cat. If you try to coax it or call it, it will avoid you. It will never come. But if you pay no attention to it and go about your business, you'll find it rubbing up against your legs and jumping into your lap.

WILLIAM BENNETT

When you're special to a cat, you're special indeed. . .she brings to you the gift of her preference of you, the sight of you, the sound of your voice, the touch of your hand.

LEONORE FLEISHER

Of all domestic animals the cat is the most expressive. His face is capable of showing a wide range of expressions. His tail is a mirror of his mind. His gracefulness is surpassed only by his agility. And, along with all these, he has a sense of humor.

WALTER CHANDOHA

Balancing, teetering, seemingly never
afraid of the fall from the fence or the rail
or the highest cabinet in the kitchen. Slight
of step and nimble beyond imagination,
weaving between the precious items on the
bureau but not displacing one. No circus
act holds such suspense and grace as
my cat in her wanderings.

CAROL SMITH

*Be glad in the Lord and rejoice, you righteous;
and shout for joy, all you upright in heart!*

PSALM 32:11 NKJV

*So the ransomed of the Lord shall return, and
come to Zion with singing, with everlasting
joy on their heads. They shall obtain joy and
gladness; sorrow and sighing shall flee away.*

ISAIAH 51:11 NKJV

*Long ago your own people did these same
things to the prophets. So when this happens
to you, be happy and jump for joy! You will
have a great reward in heaven.*

LUKE 6:23 CEV

*Evil people are trapped by sin, but the
righteous escape, shouting for joy.*

PROVERBS 29:6 NLT

What a treat it is to see cats lie upside down and bump their rumps from side to side. I think it means they have just won the lottery. I always check in the cat bed for a winning stub.

INGRID NEWKIRK

Apparently, through scientific research, it has been determined that a cat's affection gland is stimulated by snoring, thus explaining my cat's uncontrollable urge to rub against my face at 2 a.m.

TERRI L. HANEY

Most pets display so many humanlike traits and emotions it's easy to forget they're not gifted with the English language and then get snubbed when we talk to them and they don't say anything back.

STEPHENIE GEIST

My cat exhibits all kinds of behavior normally associated with dogs. He fetches and retrieves sticks, understands and reacts to commands, chases people and dogs down the street, and eats all sorts of things that cats shouldn't like. Do I have a cat? Or is he a dog in disguise?

CAROL SMITH

I love cats because I love my home and after a while they become its visible soul.

JEAN COCTEAU

167

*If you are cheerful, you feel good;
if you are sad, you hurt all over.*

PROVERBS 17:22 CEV

*All the days of the desponding and
afflicted are made evil [by anxious
thoughts and forebodings], but he who
has a glad heart has a continual feast
[regardless of circumstances].*

PROVERBS 15:15 AMP

*Our LORD, let your worshipers rejoice and be
glad. They love you for saving them, so let
them always say, "The LORD is wonderful!"*

PSALM 40:16 CEV

*My lips will shout for joy when I sing
praise to you—I whom you have delivered.*

PSALM 71:23 NIV

I love my little kitty
Her coat is so warm.
And if I don't hurt her
She'll do me no harm.
I won't pull her tail,
Or drive her away
And kitty and I
Very gently will play.

MOTHER GOOSE

Do you see that kitten chasing so prettily her own tail? If you could look with her eyes, you might see her surrounded with hundreds of figures performing complex dramas, with tragic and comic issues, long conversations, many characters, many ups and downs of fate.

RALPH WALDO EMERSON

Give thanks to the LORD, for he is good! His faithful love endures forever. Cry out, "Save us, O God of our salvation! Gather and rescue us from among the nations, so we can thank your holy name and rejoice and praise you." Praise the LORD, the God of Israel, who lives from everlasting to everlasting! And all the people shouted "Amen!" and praised the LORD.

1 CHRONICLES 16:34–36 NLT

Worship the LORD with gladness. Come before him, singing with joy.

PSALM 100:2 NLT

171

Cats are way above begging for food.
Cats prefer the direct approach when
it comes to getting our fair share—
by being yowling, insufferable pests,
or just hopping up and helping ourselves.

JOE GARDEN

Cats speak a subtle language in which
few sounds carry many meanings,
depending on how they are sung or
purred. "Mnrhnh" means comfortable
soft chairs. It also means fish. It means
genial companionship. . .and the
absence of dogs.

VAL SCHAFFNER

Who would believe such
pleasure from a wee ball o' fur?

IRISH SAYING

My Brother,
My Cat

One who has unreliable friends soon comes to ruin, but there is a friend who sticks closer than a brother.

PROVERBS 18:24 NIV

After a serious accident and surgery, my husband was laid up for several weeks nursing his ankle. Accustomed to being very active, he didn't enjoy sitting around. Eventually, his inactivity would get the best of him, and he'd hobble around the house using a walker. Almost always, his foot would start to hurt and swell, and back to the couch he'd go to elevate his ankle on a pillow. Without fail, at least two of the cats would hop on the sofa, with one of them making a nest beside my husband, sometimes falling asleep beside him.

It seems our cats always know when we don't feel well. Their presence warms and comforts us as they minister to our souls with their soft fur and loud purrs. They do not judge us, but simply give of themselves to make us feel better.

Am I always an unselfish person to those I am friends with? I'm urged by my cats' example to be a better friend to my human companions.

Few things bring out the passion in people like cats. Many humans adore felines as they adore no other creature. There is an intimacy to cats—a club only they can invite you to join. It is the feeling that I am a trusted and special friend, fully sanctioned to enter a private world.

SARA WILSON

A cat is a very special friend who comes into your life. When it comes it brings warmth, companionship, contentment, and love. Whether it's long-haired, short-haired, pedigreed or "heinz" makes no difference. A cat, though independent, has a way of letting you know that without you life just wouldn't be worthwhile.

SHARON LUNDBLAD

May there always be a cat to comfort you when you are sad, to amuse you when you are bored, to keep you company when you are lonely, to remind you that a nap in the sun is a fine thing, and to show you that the natural world is always just a purr and a pounce away.

BRIAN KILCOMMONS AND SARA WILSON

Christ encourages you, and his love comforts you. God's Spirit unites you, and you are concerned for others.

PHILIPPIANS 2:1 CEV

Even though I walk through the darkest valley, I will fear no evil, for you are with me; your rod and your staff, they comfort me.

PSALM 23:4 NIV

Remember your promise to me; it is my only hope. Your promise revives me; it comforts me in all my troubles.

PSALM 119:49–50 NLT

Nevertheless God, who comforts the downcast, comforted us.

2 CORINTHIANS 7:6 NKJV

A dog will show his love by jumping on you at the front door. A cat will show his love by ignoring you, and then curling up next to you when you need it most.

DANIELLE ASSON

A cat can be trusted to purr when she is pleased, which is more than can be said for human beings.

WILLIAM RALPH INGE

A small, four-legged, fur-bearing extortionist.
A wildlife control expert impersonator.
An unprogrammable animal.
A four footed allergen.
A hair relocation expert.
A treat-seeking missile.
A lapwarmer with a built-in buzzer.
A small, furry lap fungus.

GANDEE VASAN

Show me a sign for good, that those who hate me may see it and be ashamed, because You, Lord, have helped me and comforted me.

PSALM 86:17 NKJV

I find true comfort, Lord, because your laws have stood the test of time.

PSALM 119:52 CEV

Praise be to the God and Father of our Lord Jesus Christ, the Father of compassion and the God of all comfort, who comforts us in all our troubles, so that we can comfort those in any trouble with the comfort we ourselves receive from God. For just as we share abundantly in the sufferings of Christ, so also our comfort abounds through Christ.

2 CORINTHIANS 1:3–5 NIV

At times, cats seem like hairy little people. In times of sickness or sorrow they may wrap your head in their paws, nuzzle your neck, or lick your cheek. A calm atmosphere is deeply linked to survival. If you are upset or ill, your cat will do whatever it takes to soothe you, so that his home becomes secure once more.

ERIC SWANSON

The purr is at the heart of our close relationship with the cat. However, there are few early historical references to purring. One does occur in the eulogy to Beland the cat, written by Joachim du Bellay in the mid-sixteenth century: He was my favorite plaything/And not forever purring/A long and timeless/Grumbling litany.

ROGER TABOR

When you've been working too hard,
a cat will walk across your papers to let
you know it's time for a break. A cat will
show his gratitude for the simplest act,
such as scratching him under the chin,
by serenading you with his deep, rich purr.
A cat will still adore you on those days
when you look your worst.

PAM JOHNSON-BENNETT

Though you have made me see troubles, many and bitter, you will restore my life again; from the depths of the earth you will again bring me up. You will increase my honor and comfort me once more.

PSALM 71:20–21 NIV

Teach them to do everything I have told you. I will be with you always, even until the end of the world.

MATTHEW 28:20 CEV

I can rarely remember having passed a cat in the street without stopping to speak to it.

BRUCE MARSHALL

Cat lovers can readily be identified. Their clothes always look old and well used. Their sheets look like bath towels and their bath towels look like a collection of knitting mistakes.

ERIC GURNEY

If you're lucky enough to own a cat consider yourself one of life's winners because when you have a cat around you'll never be lonely; the sound of its purr will give you comfort, and as you hold it and pet it, stress will slip away.

SHARON LUNDBLAD

If you took a poll among cat owners, an overwhelming number of them would tell you that they hadn't been looking for a cat, hadn't planned on one, and maybe didn't even care much for cats—the feline love of their lives just walked in. More often than not, it's the cats who choose us.

PAM JOHNSON-BENNETT

Although all cat games have their rules and rituals, these vary with the individual player. The cat, of course, never breaks a rule. If it does not follow precedent, that simply means it has created a new rule and it is up to you to learn it quickly if you want the game to continue.

SIDNEY DENHAM

Cats nurture, watch over, and play with us as if we were babes who didn't know how to take care of ourselves—and certainly didn't have a clue about when to indulge in a rollicking good time.

ALLEN AND LINDA ANDERSON

187

*I serve you, L*ORD*. Comfort me with your love, just as you have promised.*

PSALM 119:76 CEV

"God blesses those who mourn, for they will be comforted."

MATTHEW 5:4 NLT

Finally, brethren, farewell. Become complete. Be of good comfort, be of one mind, live in peace; and the God of love and peace will be with you.

2 CORINTHIANS 13:11 NKJV

If you are tired from carrying heavy burdens, come to me and I will give you rest.

MATTHEW 11:28 CEV

A cat's love may seem hard won at times,
but oh, the sweetness of the unguarded
feline heart which has been won over.
It takes a certain amount of time and
attention that creates the kind of safety
that a kitty's heart revels in.

**Independent as they are, cats find
more than pleasure in our company.**

LLOYD ALEXANDER

Cats have a curious effect on people. They seem to excite more extreme sentiments than any other animals. There are people who cannot remain in the room with a cat—who feel instinctively the presence of a cat even though they do not actually see it. On the other hand, there are people who, whatever they may be doing, will at once get up and fondle a cat immediately [when] they see it.

ARTHUR PONSONBY

Cats are admirable company. I am very fond of dogs, too; but their sphere is the field. In the house they do not understand that repose of manner which is the soul of breeding. The cat's manners or rather manner seems to have been perfected by generations, nay centuries, of familiar intercourse with the great and cultivated of the earth.

ALGERNON S. LOGAN

You should have seen her. Cutest little pixie face with big beautiful eyes. . .a cute little turned-up nose. . .luxuriant curly hair. . .and big old ears that would put Spock to shame. Needless to say, I was smitten.

CAROL SMITH

About the Author

Betty Ost-Everley is an animal lover. From the first time she laid eyes on a cuddly kitten, she was hooked. A parent to three formerly feral cats, when Betty's not working as an administrative assistant, she divides her time between family, church, her neighborhood, writing, and crafting.